Copyright 2017

Table of Contents

Introduction

Personal Finance Tips

Invest

401(k) and 403(b) Plans

Types of Mutual Funds

Stock Research

The Powers of Compounding Money

The Powers of Compounding Money II

Insurance

Automobile Insurance

Renters and Homeowners Policy Insurance

Umbrella Insurance

Disability Insurance

Life Insurance

Summary

Additional Resources

DISCLAIMER: this book is not intended to be construed as investment advice.

To my family and friends

'Rule No.1: Never lose money. Rule No.2: Never forget rule No.1'

~ **Warren Buffett**

Introduction

This book compiles is about personal finance and is not only helpful to the beginner, but also to the expert. The methods and techniques described and discussed herein are fairly easy to understand and to follow-through with.

This book will also discuss some of the types of mutual funds and workplace-sponsored retirement plans. Also, the powers of compounding money is discussed. Lastly, a section on insurance is included

Personal Finance Tips

RULE #1: **NEVER LOSE MONEY.**

In essence, SAVE! That is, do not spend more money than what you earn. To quote billionaire hotelier, restauranteur and Houston Rockets owner, Tilman Fertitta:

"SO FIRST THING, MORE THAN ANYTHING, KNOW YOUR NUMBERS"

Ensure that your income doesn't exceed your living expenses. Visualize the equation below:

<u>INCOME - EXPENSES = PROFIT</u>

Remember RULE #1!

RULE #2 – **NEVER FORGET RULE #1!**

RULE #3 – **PAY YOURSELF FIRST!**

Next, after spending money on necessary expenses such as a mortgage, rent, insurance, utilities, discretionary items, entertainment and fun, save as much as you can.

With those savings, enroll into an automatic savings plan and have the money deposited into your checking or savings account at your bank or credit union. Do this once a month. In five, ten, twenty years from now you will thank yourself for doing so.

Investing

Invest

Next invest your savings by dollar cost averaging into mutual funds or stocks that have a good track record and low expense ratios. Dollar-cost-averaging is investing a set amount of money (for example, $100.00) every week, two weeks or month. The purpose of dollar-cost-averaging is to even out the peaks and troughs of stock market movements.

Mutual funds are investment vehicles that pool and manage money from investors. Mutual funds invest the money into the stock and / or bond markets.

To find a mutual fund with a good track record, you can find the rates of returns by reading the mutual fund's prospectus. Prospectuses are documents that show what stocks and / or bonds that the mutual funds are holding. They also show what rates of returns that a mutual fund has made over a period of time (one year, two years, five years, ten years; even the life of the fund). Compare those returns to the other mutual funds offered by your employer and diversify your money among the best performing mutual funds offered or diversify your money among the mutual funds that best suit your needs.

401(k) and 403(b) Plans

If your employer offers a workplace sponsored retirement plan such as a 401(k) or 403(b) that have mutual funds, enroll in it as soon as you can. Essentially that is a bonus that you should take advantage of; because your employer will match your contribution dollar for dollar up to a certain percentage of gross income. Enroll in the plan and invest, dollar-cost-average, automatically during each bi-weekly pay period.

As mentioned, many workplace retirement plans match dollar-for-dollar what you save and invest, up to 6% of gross income in many cases. For example, if your gross income is $2,000.00 a pay period, you can invest up to 6% (or $120) a pay period and your company will match the amount, $120.00. Your employer will typically offer a list of mutual funds available for selection in the prospectus that is provided by the company managing the mutual funds.

Look at each mutual fund in the prospectus to determine the best rates of returns and expense ratios. Diversify your money among the best available funds or the ones that suit your needs and objectives, which will be explained in the following section

Types of Mutual Funds

Mutual funds can be divided into three classes; growth funds, income funds and hybrid funds. Each one of these funds can suit different needs for different individuals.

A growth fund will generally invest in just stocks. With a growth fund, it is best to invest your money in it for a long period of time, such as over five years or more. Over the long run, growth funds will outperform income and hybrid funds, however, they are more risky and volatile in the short term.

An income fund typically invests in bonds or high paying, yielding, dividend stocks. Income funds are less risky than growth and hybrid funds. Income funds regularly pay out interest and / or dividends once a month or every quarter (for example, every three months); hence income funds are generally more stable than growth and hybrid funds, but have less potential for price appreciation.

Some mutual funds are classified as hybrid funds; that is, they have the characteristics of both growth funds and income funds. Those funds are typically less volatile than growth funds and more volatile than income funds. They are suited to the investor who wants some stock market appreciation as well as interest and dividend payouts

Stock Research

If you like to do stock research analysis, buy an investment research manual called the Value Line Investment Survey manual. The Value Line Investment Survey manual is published by Value Line, Inc., based out of New York City, and tracks the common stocks of well over two-thousand companies.

The Value Line Survey manual provides historic financial information, dating back to as much as fifteen years. It offers stock charts, financial ratios (earning per share, price-to-earnings ratios, operating margins, dividend yields, dividend payouts, debt ratios, and more) and opinions from analysts about the company. The survey also groups and categorizes companies by every industry imaginable (banks, internet, oil, restaurants, grocery stores, retail / clothing stores, to name a few). The Value Line Investment Survey manual can be purchased at valueline.com. A subscription can run as high as several hundred dollars a year

The Powers of Compounding Money

Also understand the powers of compounding money. Depending upon the rate of return and time (e.g., years) that you have to invest, your money can grow significantly. For example, if you start today with $10,000.00, and the money that you invest compounds at a rate of 5% a year, in twenty years you will have around **$25,000.00**. But since 5% is a conservative return, image the following scenarios:

- If you start today with $10,000.00, and the money that you invest compounds at a rate of 10% a year, in twenty years you will have around **$61,000.00**.

- If you start today with $10,000.00, and the money that you invest compounds at a rate of 15% a year, in twenty years you will have around **$142,000.00**.

- If you start today with $10,000.00, and the money that you invest compounds at a rate of 20% a year, in twenty years you will have around **$319,000.00!**

- Or if you start today with $10,000.00, and the money that you invest compounds at a rate of 25% a year, in twenty years you will have around **$693,000.00!**

- Or take an extreme example: if you start today with $10,000.00, and the money that you invest compounds at a rate of 50% a year, in forty years you will have around **$73,715,548,806.27!**

* Please note that these scenarios assume no added money and capital, and assumes no taxes.

The Powers of Compounding Money II

How about if you add $500.00 a month, or $1,000.00 a month in addition to the $10,000.00 that you started out with? If you start today with $10,000.00, add $500.00 a month to invest, and the money that you invest compounds at an annual rate of 10% a year, in twenty years you will have around **$89,000.00**.

If you start today with $10,000.00, add $500.00 a month to invest, add $500.00 a month to invest, and the money that you invest compounds at an annual rate of 15% a year, in twenty years you will have around **$193,000.00**.

If you start today with $10,000.00, add $500.00 a month to invest, and the money that you invest compounds at an annual rate of 20% a year, in twenty years you will have around **$412,000.00!**

Or if you start today with $10,000.00, add $500.00 a month to invest, and the money that you invest compounds at an annual rate of 25% a year, in twenty years you will have around **$864,000.00!**

Or take an extreme example: if you start today with $10,000.00, add $500.00 a month to invest, and the money that you invest compounds at an annual rate of 50% a year, in forty years you will have around

$84,772,879,627.21!

Based on the scenarios above, some of the hypothetical outcomes are below if you add $1,000.00 a month:

If you start today with $10,000.00, add $1,000.00 a month to invest, and the money that you invest compounds at an annual rate of 10% a year, in twenty years you will have around **$117,000.00.**

If you start today with $10,000.00, add $1,000.00 a month to invest and the money that you invest compounds at an annual rate of 15% a year, in twenty years you will have around **$243,000.00**.

If you start today with $10,000.00, add $1,000.00 a month to invest and the money that you invest compounds at an annual rate of 20% a year, in twenty years you will have around **$505,000.00!**

Or if you start today with $10,000.00, add $1,000.00 a month to invest and the money that you invest compounds at an annual rate of 25% a year, in twenty years you will have around **$1,035,000.00!**

Or take an extreme example: if you start today with $10,000.00, add $1,000.00 a month to invest and the money that you invest compounds at an annual rate of 50% a year, in forty years you will have around

$73,715,548,806.27!

Again, please note that these scenarios assume that there is no added money and capital, and also assumes no taxes.

There are also two books available on compounding money (The Powers of Compounding Money and also The Powers of Compounding Money II) at the links that follow. Detailed charts are available that show how much one can make over a long period of time with a small amount of money at varying rates of returns. The first book is for beginners and the second book discusses more advanced topics, the links for the books follow:

The Powers of Compounding Money

http://amzn.to/2wGXTJ9

The Powers of Compounding Money II

http://amzn.to/2wJmBH5

Compounding money is a great way to earn passive income without having to actively work.

Insurance

Automobile Insurance

Many states require automobile insurance coverage. To protect yourself, and others, you must have a plan. Below are the types of coverages available on a typical automobile policy plan:

Bodily Injury

If you hurt someone in an auto accident.

Property Damage Liability

If you damage someone else's property in an auto accident.

Uninsured Motorists Bodily Injury

If an uninsured or underinsured driver injures you or your passengers.

Uninsured Motorist Property Damage

If an uninsured or underinsured driver damages your vehicle.

Medical Expense Benefits

If you or your passengers are injured in an auto accident.

Income-Loss Benefits

If you or your passengers are injured in an auto accident and have lost income from not being able to work.

Other Than Collision

Covers damage caused by something other than another vehicle such as hail, theft, or collision with an animal.

Collision

Covers damage to your vehicle caused by impact with an object other than an animal.

Car Replacement Assistance

If your vehicle is declared a total loss, we'll pay you an additional.

Accident Forgiveness

Stop a future accident from increasing your premium. This feature applies to only one at-fault accident per policy at a time.

Transportation

Pays for a rental vehicle while yours is being repaired due to a covered loss.

Towing and Labor

Provides emergency roadside assistance (such as towing, flat tire changing and delivery of gas).

Renters and Homeowners Policy Insurance

In addition to auto insurance, one should obtain a renters or homeowners policy depending upon ones living situation. The following list some of the coverages that are covered under a homeowners insurance policy:

Dwelling - Building Items

For condos, dwelling means the part of the building you are responsible for, which is sometimes referred to as building items or additions and alterations. Materials used for construction such as lumber and drywall, or for finishing the interior of the property, such as electrical outlets or lighting and plumbing fixtures. The limit reflects the amount of coverage you'll have for these items if your unit is destroyed by a covered event.

Personal Belongings

Personal belongings refers to all of your belongings and household goods.

Loss of Use

This covers the necessary increase in living expenses incurred by you so that your household can maintain its normal standard of living when you are unable to live in your home as a result of a covered loss. Payment will be for the shortest time required to repair or replace the damage, or if you permanently relocate, the shortest time required for your household to settle elsewhere.

Personal Liability — Each Occurrence

Personal Liability provides protection if someone makes a claim or files a suit against you (or someone covered by the policy) for accidental bodily injury or property damage and the cost to defend any such claims or suits against you. Your limit of coverage should be high enough to protect the total value of your personal assets, including your home. Example: if someone slips and falls on your property and sues you, this coverage would protect you.

Medical Payments to Others

This coverage provides medical expenses for people other than you and your family who may be injured either on your premises or as a result of your actions away from the home. Refer to your policy documents for complete details.

Flood

Flood means any flood, surface water, waves, tidal water, overflow of a body of water, or spray from any of these, whether or not driven by wind.

Other Covered Perils

This is the amount your loss must exceed in order for your policy to begin paying for covered losses other than earthquake. Refer to your policy documents for complete details.

Wind and Hail

This is the amount that damage to your home caused by wind and hail must exceed for your policy to begin paying. For example: If you have a $1,000 deductible and hail causes $3,000 of damage to your home; your policy would pay $2,000 and you would have to pay the first $1,000. If your deductible is a percentage, it is based on your dwelling limit and will vary as this limit changes.

The following exceptions apply:

Homeowner condominiums and co-ops (deductible is based on your personal property limit)

Rental property condominiums and co-ops (deductible is based on your building items limit)

In Maryland effective October 1, 2008, the wind and hail deductible will only apply to hurricane losses.

Please note that companies that issue homeowners policies may have different coverages or different names.

Umbrella Insurance

If you have significant assets then it would be a good idea to purchase an umbrella insurance policy. Umbrella insurance is also known as extra liability insurance.

Umbrella insurances is designed to help protect and cover you from major claims and lawsuits and as a result it helps protect your assets and your future. It does this in two ways: provides additional liability coverage above the limits of your homeowners, auto, and boat.

Disability Insurance

Disability is an illness or injury, either physical or mental, which prevents you from performing your regular and customary work. Disability includes elective surgery, pregnancy, childbirth, or related medical conditions.

Although work-related disabilities are covered by workers' compensation laws, disability insurance benefits may also be paid for work-related illness or injuries under certain circumstances prescribed by law.

Life Insurance

Life insurance, is a contract between an insurance policy holder and an insurer or assurer, where the insurer promises to pay a designated beneficiary a sum of money in exchange for a premium, upon the death of an insured person.

Summary

To summarize don't forget RULEs #1, #2 and #3. Also know your numbers and save automatically. After you have paid yourself first, then invest your savings in a mutual fund or mutual funds suited to your needs.

Also take advantage of your company's 401 (k) and 403 (b) workplace sponsored retirement plans if one is offered.

Both plans offer tax breaks and matching by your employer

If you want to get into researching the financials of a company, try using the Value Line Investment Survey manual and to see and learn if a company is making money or not. Also, understand the importance of the powers of compounding money.

And lastly, be sure that you are aware of your insurance needs depending on your needs and objectives so that you are adequately protected in case of a loss or claim.

DISCLAIMER: this book is not intended to be construed as investment advice.

ADDITIONAL RESOURCES

LINKS TO BOOKS

The Powers of Compounding Money

http://amzn.to/2wGXTJ9

The Powers of Compounding Money II

http://amzn.to/2wJmBH5

AUTHOR'S YOUTUBE CHANNELS

https://www.youtube.com/channel/UCq7uNSjONd6E8tsvErAHqNQ

https://www.youtube.com/channel/UC9xoY04t1q4whrjPjf2b0Uw

AUTHOR'S BLOGS

https://thestockmarketinvestorblog.blogspot.com

https://thestockpicker2010.blogspot.com

https://stockmarketinvestorblog.blogspot.com

https://thestockpickingblog.blogspot.com

https://thevalueinvestorblog.blogspot.com

https://personalfinancetimes.blogspot.com

https://theeconomicanalyst.blogspot.com

https://mymoneymakingtipsblog.blogspot.com

https://weightlossdecrease.blogspot.com

AUTHOR'S FACEBOOK PAGE

https://facebook.com/stock.trader.39

TWITTER

@Jrlvt

LINKS TO SUPPORT THE AUTHOR'S WORK

SHOP AT THE AMAZON LINK BELOW TO SUPPORT AUTHOR'S WORK:

https://amzn.to/2gRrd9W

MAKE A PAYPAL CONTRIBUTION TO SUPPORT AUTHOR'S WORK:

https://paypal.me/JamesLynd

PERFECT THREADS CLOTHING COMPANY

Check out the author's clothing company at the link below, you can create your very own clothing / shirts; once inside the link, just click on the "CREATE' link to get started:

https://shop.spreadshirt.com/PerfectThreads

OTHER INFORMATION

The author has a Master of Business Administration degree with a concentration in Finance from the University of Baltimore and a Bachelor of Science Degree from Virginia Tech. In addition to having interests in money, investing and wealth, the author has interests in building businesses, e-commerce, sports, travel and organic gardening.

NOTES SECTION

NOTES SECTION

END

www.ingramcontent.com/pod-product-compliance
Lightning Source LLC
Chambersburg PA
CBHW050014230526
45470CB00003B/956